Arising Soul Pals:

Keep your eyes on the rise

Andrew P. Michael, AMP

BALBOA.PRESS
A DIVISION OF HAY HOUSE

Balboa Press books may be ordered through booksellers or by contacting:

Balboa Press
A Division of Hay House
1663 Liberty Drive
Bloomington, IN 47403
www.balboapress.com
844-682-1282

Because of the dynamic nature of the Internet, any web addresses or links contained in this book may have changed since publication and may no longer be valid. The views expressed in this work are solely those of the author and do not necessarily reflect the views of the publisher, and the publisher hereby disclaims any responsibility for them.

The author of this book does not dispense medical advice or prescribe the use of any technique as a form of treatment for physical, emotional, or medical problems without the advice of a physician, either directly or indirectly. The intent of the author is only to offer information of a general nature to help you in your quest for emotional and spiritual well-being. In the event you use any of the information in this book for yourself, which is your constitutional right, the author and the publisher assume no responsibility for your actions.

Print information available on the last page.

ISBN: 978-1-9822-5924-2 (sc)
ISBN: 978-1-9822-5926-6 (hc)
ISBN: 978-1-9822-5925-9 (e)

Library of Congress Control Number: 2020923105

Balboa Press rev. date: 02/26/2021

CONTENTS

PART I: Summary: Mapping the rise of Soul Pals from sea to sky
Invitation (http://bit.ly/InvitationforJust-us)

In these stories, each character is called a Pal. A Pal from each story is a bridge to the next story. With each episode in the upward spiral, the altitude of characters rise as a player's attitude can rise to a higher level of consciousness.

ACKNOWLEDGEMENT

The core of manifestation is acknowledging what you love and having confidence in what you would like more of in your life. I acknowledge with gratitude, people who taught me about the power of acknowledgement as core to creating your life. What you acknowledge thinking, seeing, feeling and hearing now grows to become how you will live in the future.

PREQUEL: The **O**ctopus's **M**agical **G**arden (OMG)

PAL Bridge: The Octopus's place of living is under attack from the environmental pollution caused by increased shipping. With allies, Coco creates a protective home she calls a garden. A pelican splashes down diving into OMG and meets the Octopus.

CHAPTER 1: *Pelican Park*: Brownie, a pelican had been born just before his mother ventured out to do some reconnaissance over the recent oil spill. Sadly, she never returned, despite exhaustive efforts to find her. Brownie was motivated to help others avoid death by tar formed by spilled oil. Pelican Park was born. In fact, just before the oil spill, an Octopus had formed a garden for fellow sea creatures to resist the onslaught of development that was erasing their habitat (Chapter 7). A pod of pelicans had just surveyed the oil spill damage while collecting food.

PAL Bridge: A pelican baths in ease at the Egret's Lagoon where he and the egret chirp and chat as the two friends enjoy a meal together.

CHAPTER 2: Listen in at the *Egret's Lagoon* as she plays at ease and strolls about. The easy nature of the egret stands next to the pelican that is always busy achieving its aims through flight, diving, soaring, gliding, and returning to land. All over the world 'cattle egret' stand upon the shoulder of large four leggeds, like the India one-horned rhino and the African elephant

PAL Bridge: The egret is present everywhere. It stands atop the African elephant as it migrates to various homes of water and vegetation.

CHAPTER 3: *Jaded in the Forest of Lake Chad* follows the steps of the elephant herd as it migrates to and from Lake Chad. There it shares a watering hole with the hippopotamus, crocodile, and once with the West African Black Rhino.

PAL Bridge: The African elephant is brother to the Asian elephant. They are on high alert for poachers in the fields it roams in India. The egret does what she can from the rhino's shoulders to be a calming force. She helps him appreciate its keen awareness about its surroundings. They are sharper and more alert, when calm, rather than tense.

CHAPTER 4: In *How the Rhino Goes Green*, the rhino, a native to northern India with the Bengal tiger, Asian elephant and hummingbirds mingle with the people in the forest. Here the people are led to bright flowers by hummingbirds that use their natural 'seeing' talent. Soon the rhino will be in danger and turning it's hide from gray to green jade, critical to its life as rifle sights are pointed at him.

PAL Bridge: The hummingbird uses its natural ability to know where it is at all times during its annual migration. This natural talent is the origin for GPS – Geographic Position System. After learning things on its northern migration, the hummingbird initiates a "Pollination Protest".

CHAPTER 5: In *Breeze Over Bramazon*, the hummingbird, lion monkey, and the blue parrot, all tree-mates in the Brazilian Amazon frantically deal with the impending doom of their home in a Brazilwood tree. Hummer gets wind of what is planned for its home from Lotus Luv, a journalist from Oklahoma visiting North Carolina. North Carolina is Hummer's northern migration home.

PAL Bridge: Lotus Luv follows her journalistic hunch to India to interview a prominent scientist that has put her own state's livelihood at risk.

CHAPTER 6: In *The Flying Rhino*, The *rhino* wins its wings at the watering hole. Lotus Luv narrates her journey that has her encounter elephants and horses from the moment she lands in New Delhi, India. Later she will meet other natives, rhinos, eagles, and crocodiles. She guides us from the ground-level of majestic, regal, and powerful beings to another world where these same beings take a journey Whereby they endanger themselves for the life of others.

CHAPTER 7: The *Octopus's Magical Garden (OMG)* is an **O**pportunity **C**enter **T**o **O**ffer **P**ractical & **U**seful Solutions. In the ocean garden you have access to depths unseen by most on land. The Octopus has an intelligence inexplicable to most, as it makes remarkable predictions that turn true. The octopus determines how it wishes to shapeshift and color coordinate in any environment to survive and thrive. The Octopus is constantly innovating with its intelligence to make life possible. In fact, the octopus has designed a table to match the characters to their unique abilities and qualities. In the text that follows, characters that are underlined describe talents from which all can benefit on the playground (Chapter 8) and in links to associated websites. These conscious attributes were confirmed by 50 notable scientists in the Cambridge

<u>Declaration on Consciousness</u>. With their diverse talents they address emotional, mental, spiritual and physical challenges. The table is a playground for life. In scientific terms this is a Periodic Table of Consciousness. {See Playground for life at Chapter 8}.

PAL Bridge: After the pelican, splashes down, the octopus brings her on to be a messenger between sentient beings of land and sea. Having been at the beginning of this upward spiral, the Octopus was in the best position to develop a comprehensive table – called a Playground. Indeed, just by living you are playing on this playground. From the *Arising Series* the Game arOZe.

CHAPTER 8: PERIODIC PLAYGROUND OF CON-SCIOUSNESS is a place to take on challenges, dangers and opportunities for growth in the 3Q dimensions of consciousness – the Qualities of your IQ (Intellectual Quotient), EQ (Emotional Quotient) and We-Q(Relationship to all): The characters in the preceding stories can be played with in your 'see-sawing' and 'see-saying' playground. It allows you to enjoy and advance your **PIES** on your own upward spiral.

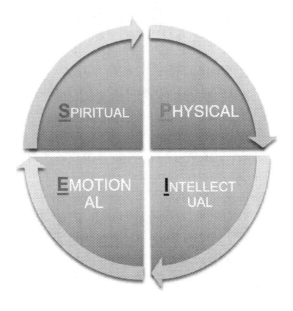

The playground has pals that you have met in the stories. They are ready and able to support growth in the **P**hysical, **I**ntellectual, **E**motional, and **S**piritual realms. On the Playground these characters have teamed up with **acti**ons and at**titudes** (actitudes) that you may apply to replenish the positive and diminish negative actitudes in yourself.

Epilogue

Arising on the upward spiral recognizes that we often meet the same characters in the same physical spaces, where we have been before. However, it is a continuous spiral upward because each time you are there in your life, you are in a new place of consciousness. Your creation of this upward spiral (us) comes down to the confidence you have in playing out your beliefs.

Propelling-confidence in your beliefs is at the base of the upward spiral. *Arising* starts with the Pelican Park. Each cycle of the spiral is completed by where you have placed the most confidence in your beliefs. Soul pals urge you to amp your upward spiral, Personally Activate Liberty and Play At Life. "You are what you eat, You are what you repeat". It is from where you arOZe that the next cycle of the spiral begins. Though the elevation and attitude on the spiral ever-rises, underneath it all is a depth of meaning that propels creation.

INVITATION

<u>Click</u> here to see the most updated and <u>colorful invitation</u>
http://bit.ly/InvitationforJust-us

You are invited to join the Jade Brigade. Join a Brazilian hummingbird's flight to a 'Pollination Protest' in the United States. Take a journey on the migration of elephants to an evaporating lake in Africa, and with a charging Rhino that turns green in India.

These stories are based on facts about people, culture, animals and the environment. The names have not been changed to protect anyone, as is often done in stories based on fact. Many mysteries are solved:

1. Why have pollinators stopped pollinating plants to grow? Why have so many bees died in recent years?
2. Why do elephants continue to migrate to Lake Chad even though it has shrunk to a mere puddle of its former grandeur (It is 5% of the size it was 50 years ago.)?
3. Why do deeply held cultural and spiritual beliefs determine the life and death of elephants and rhinos;

not food, not water, not villagers, not farmers, not herders, not even rifles? Why do rhinos reappear in Lake Chad after being declared extinct?

In these stories, the hummingbird, elephants, rhino, hippopotamus and Mamba Patrol are members of the 'Jade Brigade'. These star characters have three qualities (3Q): 1. Heart- EQ (Emotional Quotient) love and compassion, 2. Intelligence - IQ (Intellectual Quotient), and 3. Courage - WE-Q (Whole Experience of Respecting All - Quotient) - courage to do the right thing with everyone and every being in all situations.

With the power of these 3 Qualities (3Qs) on their migration, the characters could rise to the challenge and reach their goal: protecting themselves, family, friends and their homes. With these 3 Qualities (3Qs) they are able to arrive and thrive: $1EQ + 1IQ + 1WE\text{-}Q = 3Q$.

The *Arising* characters are on an 'upward spiral'. In each successive story, characters live in higher altitudes, just as readers can live in higher attitudes. These perceptions about how we experience life are formed from a rising consciousness born from the heart's love, the brain's intelligence, and acts of courage to relate to all with affection and respect, regardless of consequences.

Join the Jade Brigade anywhere in the Arising Stories and rise from the depths of the sea to the heights of the sky.

We continuously rise to higher rungs on the upward spiral.

When we reach a new level, we can recognize and name the experience to which we 'arOZe'. Going from 'arising' to having 'arOZe' is a key ingredient to creating and manifesting. This is the journey of the upward spiral where we continuously rise to new levels of consciousness, and live on that plateau for a time, until we arise again.

If we can feel it, see it and experience that to which we aspire, the future eventually becomes the present. You can live what you imagined. Albert Einstein once said, "the imagination is a preview of things to come."

From the Arising series the Game arOZe. By playing arOZe we expand our 3Q powers within to manifest what we desire at home. Home is where the heart is and where we physically live. The motto of Game arOZe is "Play-Because there is no place like home." If we play at ease, each day we can recreate (re-create) our life, as we imagine it to be. Each person plays this creation game as naturally as breathing.

As dawn breaks wherever you are, welcome to the migration on the upward spiral. You can hear it now, 'Morning has Broken' (https://youtu.be/h5D3LEjGF8A) by Eleanor Flapieod and Cat Stevens (Yusuf Islam).

You are invited to see Arising stories as a way for people of all ages to play together and rise together.

ACKNOWLEDGEMENTS

Definition of Acknowledgement as a Verb and a Noun:

To recognize the truth of what is good and amplifying it to help cause more of that to happen in your life. I acknowledge and thank with gratitude those that have taught me so much on this journey – the upward spiral.

Acknowledgement is defined and taught by Serge King, *Aloha Spirit*, Michael Wyman, Counselor, my Dad, Kenneth R. Michael, and Mom, Shelah Saul Michael - parents, Hope Hook and Pame Schmider – sisters, friends and mentors by their example. Especially influential and inspiring to me in the historical, political and economic realms are Harriet Tubman, Nelson Mandela, Lech Walesa, President Jimmy Carter, Final leader of the Soviet Union Mikhail Gorbachev who melted The Cold War by peacefully dissolving the U.S.S.R.. And to the visionary behind the "cloud", Marc Benioff who has infused spiritual values at the core of his company, Salesforce. He has truly created a global 'care force'. Thank you to Jackie Miller, personal partner with a passion for compassion and the abolition of cruelty to people, animals, and the environment, and the best partner in love and marriage. And to the best of friends met during university at UCLA, Laurie Shapiro Earp, Doug Bystry and Kip Shuman, and Deborah Pearl met during U.C. Hastings College of the Law, and Eytan Salinger who teaches me the power of music and song, stories, and mapping to reflect the perception of ourselves in community and the globe. Each has shown by their life's path, expressions of love as a way to manifest, each in their own way. I love my sisters, Pame Michael Schmider and Hope Michael Hook, who have played along with some of my musings, discoveries and who have shown extraordinary love in how they live.

Many sentient beings in the animal and plant 'queendom' must be appreciated for teaching awareness that is the mother of acknowledgement, and the blessings it manifests. A number of Soul Pals are inspired by sentient beings from many realms, especially those living in nature.

The practice of acknowledging creation is derived from the spiritual practice of being grateful, appreciative, and understanding that we are all connected at some level. Shamans, Mayans – Carmelita from the Lacondon Rainforest, Indigenous peoples, Catholic Franciscans whom I have seen and learned much with special thanks to Sister Antoniammal, Sister Infanta, Sister Daisey and Sister Jessie of the Bon Secors Convent in Chennai, India, Pope Francis, Pope John Paul II now Saint, Father Joshstrom Kureethadam a founding leader in thought and action of the Dicastery to Promote Integral Human Development at the direction of Pope Francis,

Jewish Kabbalists, mystics, Hindus especially Paramahamsa Yogananda author of *The Science behind Affirmations*, Tibetan Buddhists most notably Lama Tenzin Choegyal, founder and director of the Children's Education Development Society (C.E.D.) and the Medium of the Oracle of Tibet, Kuten La, and to the *Hawaiian Aloha Spirit* authored by Serge King, and the African Yoruba spirit with a song about Yemaya – the African goddess of the ocean by Mirabai Ceiba - all together are 'Thundering Grace', reigning down inspiration for many of the soul pals.

The positive and negative side of acknowledgment is the power to manifest form and reality. Ironically, ignoring a certain reality, re-enforces the *ignored* reality and produces more of that to which you are ignoring. Incomplete positive thinking can practically expand the negative. Yet, the same manifestation principles of acknowledgment apply to bringing in positive reality, as well. In the negative, whatever is resisted actually persists, affirming and producing what one does not like. Ultimately, Acknowledgment Manifests Perception (AMP); "Be the Cause, Cause Reality!"

PREQUEL

The **OCTOPUS's** *Magical Garden (**OMG**)* is an **O**pportunity **C**enter **T**o **O**ffer **P**ractical & **U**seful **S**olutions. Here, you access the depths of the ocean, a hidden view from what we normally see. The story of *the Octopus's Magical Garden* comes about as an imperative for the Octopus to save itself and others. Its home in the coast of Louisiana in the Gulf of Mexico has been changing. The degradation of its habitat threatens its very survival. Sea-faring cargo vessels and the oil drilled, leaked and taken from under their tentacles is flooding into water. Creating change for the habitat of the Octopus comes through actual laws of protection that come about in partnership with people. In its own way the Octopus, a sentient conscious being, finds ways to address these challenges. It is from the depths of the ocean that this journey begins and it will be from the depths of understanding that a code will be revealed for exceptional living. The *Arising* stories and their real characters face facts that are just as true to them as to us.

It is said that the end is in the beginning, and this circular cycle is also true in the Arising Stories. The whole is in the smallest of parts, one DNA code holds the blueprint for the whole being. A drop of water when magnified shows elegant crystal patterns that are the very same as snowflakes, a leaf reveals miniature pathways that mimic grand watersheds where all rivers flow into the ocean. And in *Arising* we begin with the pelican that dove into the Octopus's Magical Garden.

PAL Bridge: A symbiotic relationship with Coco - the Octopus, has resulted in daily 'underwater' reconnaissance missions by the pelican pod, to assure the healthy garden, thrives. The pelican is a messenger delivery service for the gardeners of the *Octopus's Magical Garden (OMG).*

CHAPTER 1

PELICAN PARK

Beginning: Waves of creatures are caked in black tar that tide brings to the shores of the Gulf of Mexico.

Brownie – a pelican, and the state bird of Louisiana, was defiant as oil washed tarred fish and birds to the shore. A gushing oil well had blown it's top in the Gulf of Mexico. The oil well endlessly spit-up tar, placing the lives of many of the Gulf's creatures at risk. The company, British Petroleum (BP,) was responsible for the largest oil spill ever in the world. It would be weeks before the well would be capped.

A pelican pod did large scale reconnaissance of the situation. Sometimes, like a plane flying its mission, a pelican miscalculates the amount of energy it needs to return to its home base. Sadly a few in the pod had done that, landed to rest along their return before it was safe from the oil tsunami. And some of them, sadly, were never seen again.

Middle: A refuge is created to save lives. To many, the pelican's 'can do' spirit makes Brownie their pal for survival.

1

For short they call Brownie, <u>PELICAN1PAL</u> (see http://tinyurl. com/PELICAN1PAL),

Brownie, a pelican of this pod, was not going to let this stuff snuff out him, any more of his family, and friends. Teaming with an innate confidence that life must prevail, Brownie set to building Pelican Park as a refuge for creatures to thrive, inspite of the deluge of oil.

A pack of animals took up Brownie's torch to give life a chance. Wolves provided a model for banding together so that each being that wanted to live in the Park could do so. The wolf pack creed, "United we stand, divided we fall," came to be so.

Katrina, a once a century severe hurricane had hit before the oil tsunami. Park residents themselves are refugees from the oil tsunami that ravaged the Gulf Coast courtesy of British Petroleum (BP). In the journey to resilience, some of the animals had escaped from a drowning zoo. The Panda methodically showed patience to avoid 'panda-moniam' and find a way to live. In fact, an egret did much the same going about its life with ease and avoiding self-destruction that comes from stress and panic. The egret's motto is "Don't regret, egret. Don't regret, egret."

End:

Each day Edie – the egret – had much to do to arrange care and relaxation for those living in Pelican Park. Edie - provides relaxation in her lagoon for drop-in caregivers. A cycle of care has been completed from Octopus, to Pelican, to Egret.

CHAPTER 2

EGRET'S LAGOON

After a full day of attending to Pelican Park and all the beings that live in the refuge, Brownie drifts leisurely in the lagoon. The Egret having tended to its own lagoon takes a few moments to reflect with Brownie on its day.

These 'Cattle Egret', as they are known, sit atop the water buffaloes' shoulder in the lagoon and groom them occasionally as they pick off unwanted critters on their hosts. The water buffaloes were also sauntering in the lagoon having had a full day of working with the farmer till rice fields. Indeed, the water buffalo has made life significantly easier for the farmer who used to wade into the water and do the tilling and mixing of soil by hand.

The egret relayed to the pelican that life would be a lagoon of ease if all did their calling and listened to their own cycles that include relaxation and play. In the egret's own world, Edie has a natural walk with a gate of elegant relaxation that she does with efficiency to swoop up a meal as it becomes available at its feet. She simply leaves an area that has nothing more to offer, and saunters with elegant posture to a more abundant place of food. The egret knows when to egress and avoid the gnawing irritant of expectations unfulfilled.

PAL bridge: Egrets observe and practice ease. They perch on the shoulders of magnificent beings, such as the water buffalo and the rhino, to serve them and observe them. They are the easy riders of our time.

CHAPTER 3

JADED IN THE FOREST OF LAKE CHAD

Disclaimer: *Based on facts about people, animals, and nature; the names have not been changed to protect everyone*

A strange thing happened on the way to Lake Chad. Water is draining from it due to increased irrigation and climate change. Today, it is only about 5% as large as it was in the 1960s. Of course, voracious grazers would find greener pastures elsewhere, right? Nope, in the wake of water retreating, verdant greenery grows abundantly on the lakebed. The water table from below and the rainy season from above make this soil perfect for plant and tree growth, a haven for grazers.

The view of Lake Chad made it a popular place for people to live. The lake view from years ago had now become a forest of Lake Chad. For some illuminating photos see http://bit.ly/ JadedinLakeForestJust-us. A bridge from shore to shore had now become a bridge over a forest.

Andrew P. Michael, AMP

Key moments in the story

Mapping the Journey of the Elephants

In the capital of Chad, N'Djamena ("place of rest" in Arabic) the African Park Organization has a conference to share best practices. Mamba Patrols presented the outcomes of their work to protect ivory bearing animals from hungry poachers. They use sound and visual technology to protect African elephants (See Place -1, Map p.12 at http://bit.ly/JadedinLakeForestJust-us).

Their territorial triangle covers the Waza National Park and the city of Ngoumba to the south in Cameroon to the northern sector of Lake Chad where Nigeria, Niger, Cameroon and Chad all meet (the apex of the NINICACH elephant triangle). The elephant herd had declined to 10% (2,200) of its original size (22,000). After only five years in the NIgeria-NIger-CAmeroon-CHad (NINICACH) elephant triangle, the patrol reports that the herds' population is on the increase. Numbers **1. – 6.** on the map will be referred to in the story so you can track where the elephant is in its journey.

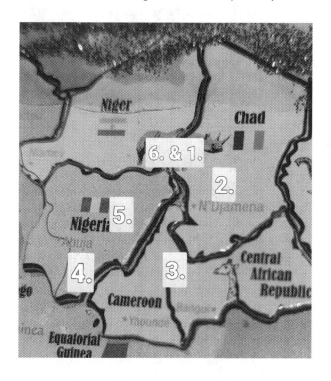

FIGURE 1 STORY MAP OF A HERD'S ANNUAL MIGRATORY PATH 1. FROM LAKE CHAD IN THE NORTH, 2. SOUTHWARD FROM

LAKE CHAD TO CAMEROON (CHINESE SURVEY TEAM POSTED HERE), ENTERING WAZA NATIONAL PARK 3. DEPARTING WAZA NATIONAL PARK TO THE RIVER MID-CAMEROON 4. PIVOT TO THE NORTHWARD RETURN MIGRATION THROUGH NORTHEASTERN NIGERIA TO 5. THE FINAL LEG THROUGH CAMEROON'S TIP, 6. COMPLETING THEIR MIGRATION IN LAKE CHAD AT THE APEX WHERE FOUR COUNTRIES MEET, NIGERIA, NIGER, CAMEROON, CHAD.

This is the journey of an elephant herd from the southern tip of Lake Chad to the plains of Cameroon and back to their northern home. NINICACH is a region of convergence of countries, people, cultures, and faith. People are drawn to the area because of its beauty and wealth of natural resources, and rare wildlife. NINICACH is an area whose name is drawn from the first two letters of the countries that intersect in Lake Chad: NIgeria, NIger, CAmeroon, CHad.

Along the migratory journey, people meet from African countries and China. African armed bands come from countries awash in guns, and whose own domestic wars have ended. These roving bands are looking to make money from anything, including the rare wildlife whose unique assets fetch high prices.

The people and their culture, language and spiritual practices interact all along the migratory path. Islam, African indigenous spiritual practices from the Yorubans and others, and Christians each co-exist and at times come into conflict. Competition over resources and control of their land and homes is a source of conflict. Each culture also holds something dear and sacred for which their reverence is obvious throughout. For instance, the name of a young calf in the elephant herd comes from an African spiritual tradition celebrating the goddess of the ocean, known as Yemaya. She was born in the lake water where the sound of the waves lapping at shore reminded many of the sounds of shore at the ocean.

Elephants, hippopotamus, crocodiles, lions, gazelles, domesticated livestock, and formerly the West African Black Rhino from Cameroon are drawn to the lake. It is a place abundant with plants and trees to graze upon and a watering hole within which to rest and refresh.

The lake is going through an emptying phase, having shrunk to a small version of its former size. This emptying of water from a lake is known as eutrophication. Chinese dam builders and canal engineers have come to 1. Northern Lake Chad and 2. land south of the lake to survey ways to increase water flow into Lake Chad. Their experience comes from building the largest hydroelectric dam project in the world, called The Three Gorges. The dam caused the resettlement of 1.2 million Chinese whose lives were uprooted by the changing depth of a lake before the dam and the altered path of the Yangtze river that flows downstream.

This story tracks the annual migration of an elephant herd where elements of nations, people, nature and notions of the sacred collide at Lake Chad. Yemaya, her mother, and the elephant herd celebrate Yemaya's first birthday at the completion of their cycle of migration from north to south and back. They had also completed their mourning of Yemaya's father who had been killed midway through their southern migration.

Preview of being Jaded in the Forest of Lake Chad

Beginning:

Cattle make their way north to the shores of Lake Chad. The rains have just begun to taper off. Farmers make sure all channels for irrigation from Lake Chad to their farmland are open and flowing. Elephants also make the trek to the shores of Lake Chad. They graze on the food that has become lush at the lake's shore. They also share in some rest and relaxation in the lake. Once called Lake Hippopotum, the Hippopotamus are swimming about, too.

Middle:

As the migration of the elephants occurs, poachers from Africa and China have also made their way to Lake Chad. The poachers hop-scotch undetected, as they make their way through various African countries to land at the shores of Lake Chad. The herd was on the move from the southern grassland plains of Cameroon. Patrols protecting the elephants had staked out pressure points along the journey to physically protect the elephants from poachers. The poachers made their bet that they could outsmart the patrols by quietly going to the shores of Lake Chad. Using reverse psychology, they knew that the Patrols assumed poachers wouldn't go to the most popular gathering site for herds at the lake. In the herds final push, they walked through lush green vegetation that filled in the lakebed where water had once prevailed.

End:

A war cry from a Hippopotamus alerts the elephant herd that poachers are on their trail. The elephants charge their way out of harm's way. However, the long arm of the rifles still could find these elephants in their high-powered sights. In their mad dash through the lush greenery, the elephants had gone green, jade to be exact, and sacred prayers reverberated in the air. DO NOT READ THE END LINES, IF YOU WISH TO DISCOVER THE MYSTERY OF WHAT HAPPENS TO YEMAYA AND HER HERD IN THE STORY THAT FOLLOWS.

Parties Converge Along the Migratory Journey

Mamba Patrols Employ Locals to Protect Wildlife

Mamba Patrols were assembled by the African Parks Organization to protect wildlife that is unique to this area and special to the world for that reason. Elephants, rhinos and others are rare and endangered as poachers take aim to sell their valuable attributes on the illegal black market. The Mamba Patrols operate in three countries of NINICACH.

The Mamba Patrol had gathered in the capitol of Chad to share best practices. They commented on the irony of their name. It refers to the powerful black mamba snake. The Islamic term for life in Arabic, 'Hayat' can be heard as the word for snake when the last consonant "T" is not said or heard. With all kinds of sound in the environment this frequently happens. Patrol two's presentation had just completed at midday. They stand as an example of providing jobs to the locals, so they need not hunt the rare animals in their midst. The Nigerian Conservation Foundation is perfecting this economic strategy for local communities in the region.

The sound of "Allah" rang out through the city from mosque minarets calling believers to midday prayer. The practice of Islam in this area of Africa is widespread and deep. It reaches into all segments of the population from farmers to families, traders to trackers of value provided by wild animals.

Paramilitary African Bands Track and Take Animals for Their Income

Bands of paramilitary composed of Africans, dart into the NINICACH elephant triangle. They are outfitted with high powered guns left over from numerous domestic conflicts in neighboring countries and their own. They are making their way to this area in search of income that can be made from poaching the high value of certain wild animals, the rhino and elephant in particular.

Chinese Develop Africa for Access to Natural Resources

A continent away, in a Chinese village of Quilin several friends and family gathered to enjoy the company of each other before a team of them would leave for Africa. Fathers and daughters, mothers and sons prayed for a safe journey. They work for ChinaPower and Bonifica who are conducting a feasibility study to build a canal from the Congo River to restore some of the waters lost from Lake Chad. The United Nations Environmental Program (UNEP) estimates 50% of the loss of lake size is due to climate and 50% is due to human activity. Yet, grazing land has increased next to the lake.

Jade statues adorn the tables and the jewelry on women and men. These Chinese revere jade because they believe it brings power, good fortune and protects them from danger. They were a team of surveyors assessing how a dam and canal could be built to replenish water into Lake Chad by funneling it from The Congo River (See Place -2., on Map, p.12 at http://bit.ly/JadedinLakeForestJust-us). They were the same survey team of Chinapower, the company that had built the largest hydropower project in the world, The Three Gorges Dam. It changed the flow of the Yangtze river. Over one million people in villages along the river were displaced. The Three Gorges Dam in China was very unpopular with these villagers. Africans in the path of this potential development are equally as wary for their homes. Hence, the Chinese travel with a security force to ward off angry villagers and protect them from seemingly dangerous animals.

The Hippopotamus Poses Biggest Human Danger

Those approaching the lake are wary of danger that lives in and around the lake. The hippopotamus is the most ferocious of foes. It appears to slowly and lazily wade in the lake and occasionally dip, submerge, sleep, and like the rhythm of breath unconsciously float to the top for a sip of air only to continue their sleep below the surface of the water. The undulating Hippo remembers things by where they are, this is called spatial cognition. Ironically, the part of the human brain that uses the syllable 'Hippo' is the Hippocampus. It resides in the temporal lobe of the brain and is known for providing spatial intelligence as well as having a role in emotions tied to the limbic system. And having "thick skin" protects the hippo from many dangers making it that much more of a formidable opponent.

Their slowness in the lake should not be taken as a sign of easy prey. On land, hippos can reach a speed of 30 mph. Their thick skin of 2 inches/6 centimeters blocks anything from the teeth and claws of crocodiles to lions and even many bullets from puncturing their skin. According to the African Yoruba culture they were called the 'elephants of the river', the Greeks called them river horses. Their thick skin is amped protection because it makes HIPPO's **H**ide **I**mpervious and **P**uncture **P**roof to **O**pposition. It is a master of *Deflecting Danger and Rebuffing Opposition.* The HIPPO inspires a message of strength to all that listen and take notice.

The hippopotamus is known as the greatest cause of death for humans from the animal world in this area. Still, Mai Mai rebels from the Congo War to this day set out for Lake Chad to poach. If cornered, the hippopotamus belts out a large war cry. It pierces whatever maybe the sounds around. Few take on hippos, even though their super canine teeth are made of ivory. Ivory fetches good money when sold on the black market. These poachers are smart and pursue other easier poaching targets.

Elephants Complete Their Annual Migratory Loop Despite the Danger

In Cameroon, near the Waza National Park and the Chari River, the elephant herd was on the move (Place -3., Map p.13). Their migration is timed to catch the high point of greenery during the short rainy season (Place - 4, Map p.12 at http://

bit.ly/JadedinLakeForestJust-us). This is an ancient migratory pathway seared into the expansive memory of these elephants. Each year the distance to the grazing fields adjacent to the shores of Lake Chad gets further away from their southernmost point. Yet as the lake shrinks, vegetation takes its place on the lakebed. Only a puddle of the former Lake Chad exists, perhaps 5% of the lakebed remains covered with water.

Motivation for the Elephant Migration to their Northern Home Despite Poachers

Yemaya was the newest member of the herd. Their return home would mark one year of life. It is a fortunate benchmark to reach for any calf, because their chances of surviving increases immeasurably.

Yemaya's mom, Jamar and much of the herd increased the pace as they neared the lake, again. The baby was one of the few bright spots in the year that had just passed. It was a bittersweet year as it was marred by the death of Yemaya's father at the midpoint of their southern migration (Place – 2., Map p.13). Poachers had tracked their migration and struck where it was least patrolled. The Mamba Patrol does its best to protect the elephants from poachers and villages threatened by plundering military-equipped poachers. However, the Mamba Patrols simply cannot cover the entire habitat of the elephants. They use technology to expand their range of protection.

These militant gangs equipped with AK-47s conduct

themselves without honor as they mimic their past acts of raping and pillaging on their way to the hunt. Many of these gangs come from places where civil wars were rampant, Congo, Sudan, Somalia and from Boko Haram in northern Nigeria.

In an odd alliance, the Chinese security forces link with the poaching gangs from Africa to protect themselves from villagers that wish to disrupt their work. Some in the Chinese security force partner with the poachers to bring back valuable ivory from the elephant and rhino tusks. It was this lethal combination that drove the West African Black Rhino into extinction declared on November 8, 2013. A postcard was printed to remember this occurrence. See the postcard, though you need not purchase the book because the this story is contained in Chapter 4, The Hunted Rhino Goes Green http://www.blurb.com/b/6230347-the-hunted-rhino-goes-on-green?ebook=531791). As China's thirst for Africa's natural resources grows, Chinese poachers are more in the field than ever. They financially are profiting from the ivory they take from wild animals and sell these animals parts on the black market.

Needless to say, the elephants were relieved to have passed through this area on their northward trek without incident (Place – 5., Map p.13). Yemaya's father's memory weighed heavily on the herd. Their return home was cause enough to celebrate. The sound of the African song named, Yemaya, could be heard as they approached Lake Chad. The song named Yemaya can be heard today. It is sung by Mirabai

Ceiba. Yemaya, the calf, was especially treasured as a symbol of life following her father's passing. The whole group had been mourning their loss when Yemaya was delivered in the waters of Lake Chad. Hippos cheered her birth too, as she was born in the shallow water much like their own calves.

A small but meaningful resurgence of elephants has happened with the introduction of the Mamba Patrol. They provide protection to the elephants and surrounding villagers. Without them, these villages are at the mercy of military equipped bands of former militants trained in senseless violence. The atrocities of past wars are now exported to neighboring countries. These terror mongers continue their ruthless pillaging of villagers, raping women and stealing valuables.

Mamba Patrols Mission: Protect Villagers and Elephants

The Mamba Patrols are trained and equipped by the African Park Organization to protect the elephants and surrounding communities from poachers. Each patrol costs an estimated $5 million, annually. The patrol mission is to protect. Patrols have been outfitted with military equipment and technology to have a fair chance against these violent bands.

Prince Harry from England funds the Mamba Patrols in three African countries. This private force has agreements with three countries to operate and manage national parks in areas where elephants and rhinos must be protected from mercenary poachers. After terrorizing local communities, they go after animals with tusks to supply the ivory market. African Park has won the support of local communities as they have provided rangers and patrol jobs to locals, as well as providing physical protection to these communities (Place – 5., Map p.13). In return, these villagers are equipped with radios and listening devices to warn the rangers and patrols of approaching poachers.

The Mamba Patrols are also culturally savvy. They use their understanding of the cultures they face to give them increased power to protect the elephants from poaching. Through knowledge of the background, language and items of reverence, they expand the range of territory they can protect. Even groups such as these militant bands have beliefs they hold in high regard. By understanding the meaning and sound of language the Mamba Patrol are anthropologists. The ambient sounds in the areas of patrol are factored into their strategy. Many of the poachers come out of a radical Islamic philosophy known as jihad and also speak Arabic. So, the Mamba Patrols fight these bands to protect people in villages and rare animals. Groups include Boko Haram in Northern Nigeria and Somalian and Sudanese refugee militants. These terrorists have been known to force their way of practicing 'jihad' Islam on others, having them submit to daily prayers. This happened recently when 200 schoolgirls, many of whom were Christian, were abducted from their school by Boko Haram.

Mamba Patrol II has tagged some of the elephants with

micro GPS listening and broadcasting devices. These micro devices act much like high tech "Ring" doorbells that protect more and more houses. The technology enables you to see, hear and broadcast to those nearby. They use this technology to keep tabs on the whereabouts of elephant herds and ward off would be poachers. From their elephant hosts, the patrols broadcast a symphony of homage to Allah and the spirit of life itself that Islamic cultures revere. The elephant foreheads are stand-ins for Mosque-like minarets, calling believers to prayer. Ominous warnings are also broadcast from these devices.

Animal Summit at the Lake's Shore

Wildlife, such as grazers like antelope and elephants, along with lions, crocodiles, hyenas and hippopotamus live in the basin. The earliest name for the lake came from the abundance of hippopotamus in the lake. The waters and the surrounding shoreline vegetation draw all sorts of wildlife and domestic herds (Place – 6., Map p.13). Due to the enormous demand for ivory, initially from Europeans and North Americans, and now Asians, the populations of elephants and rhinoceros have dramatically declined. Sadly, the demand for elephant tusks and busts has increased with the extinction of the rhinoceros in this area.

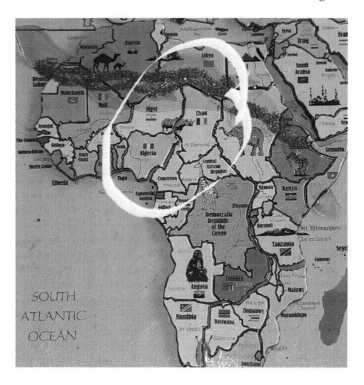

With the loss of life for animals living in the lake and loss of livelihood for approximately 10 million people whose work value is derived from the lake, tension in the area has dramatically increased. For many, the income of the past cannot be relied upon. Grazing and agriculture breed conflict as they fight for control of land and natural resources.

During the short month of the rainy season herders bring their cattle and other livestock to graze. Wild elephants, giraffe, antelope and once the West African Black Rhino, all vegetarian grazers, also make their way to these growing fields. Different motives drive the way these animals are treated. Some are welcomed and others are seen as encroachers on their land and livelihoods.

China is now the largest national investor in African countries, seeking access to Africa's natural resources. With an uptick in Chinese and Asian interest in Africa, comes more interest in the unique and prized animals living on the continent.

Yemaya, Jamar, and their whole herd finally reached the lakebed of vegetation along with cattle, elephants, giraffes, and antelopes, also grazers.

Yemaya, Jamar and the entire 'birthday party' began luxuriating in this grazing oasis. They celebrated life with Yemaya who stood as their greatest symbol. The herd had deeply felt the loss of their herd mate and were relieved and refreshed being with Yemaya. Surviving the year had been a great challenge. Finding food and water and not scaring people who kept coming closer to where they live is an ever-present experience. Their lifeline of food and water was nearing an end just when their neural networks re-cognized their need to begin their migration north to the lake. The elephant mind is known for its great memory power and for the care it shows to its family, both alive and those that have passed on. Elephants have this reputation in part because they are well attuned to ancient recall of migratory seasons. This is an amazing memory bank for the ages. Scientists have confirmed the consciousness, empathic, and intellectual capacity of elephants and many other animals (See the *Cambridge Declaration of Consciousness*).

Poachers swoop to this area knowing that water and vegetation are the best bait for their prey. They use this knowledge to exploit the interests of the farmers to keep wild animals off their land.

Herders protect their grazing areas from large wild animals that appear frightening and a danger to their food supply.

Cries for Life

All of the sudden, a loud war cry from a hippopotamus pierced the lazy afternoon.

This was a warning cry to elephants that poachers were on the hunt targeting their tusks.

In a flash, the ghost of rhinoes past appeared below the feet of the Hippo (See p12 and at http://bit.ly/JadedinLakeForestJust-us). It had reared itself up to make its cry carry as far as possible. The white ghost of the West African Black Rhino screamed to the elephants to get out of the sights of the poachers' rifles (Place – 6., Map p.13).

Immediately, Jamar pushed Yemaya to race out of the area. As they charged through the lush greenery, they became draped in the vegetation. The branches, leaves and the verdant green color rubbed onto the racing elephants. At the same time the sensors and visuals available to the Mamba Patrol were triggered – just like when a visitor that is at the door of a house. By being able to identify the danger, the small speakers attached to the elephants were activated. The calls for the Spirit of 'Allah' and 'life' itself were transmitted through the air. As fast as they moved, the elephants could not escape the long range of these killing rifles, AK-47s. Likewise, the closer the poachers came to their target, the louder the Arabic chants for

Allah and life became. They were warned to immediately leave and drop their weapons or face a barrage of gunfire.

The word "Life" can also be used as a synonym of the word "Soul" or "Spirit", in this case the Arabic word would be "حورل" = "Al Rouh". When the prefix of 'al' is silent, the remaining "Rouh" can be mistaken for "Yu". In Chinese, "Yu" means jade. Also in Arabic, the word honoring spirit ('حَيَاة' ḥayāh) comes to mean snake ('حَيَّة', ḥayyah) if the final consonant is not heard. Meaning comes to the ears based in part on what people are expecting to hear.

The elephants had become a majestic collage of jade beings in the brush. The herd huddled in a wide circle to shield Yemaya and the others most vulnerable from the danger. Eerie sounds were coming from the forest. In China, jade is revered as a powerful element that brings nourishment, good fortune, and protection. Seeing the 'jade brigade' and hearing sacred words that honor life in Arabic and jade in Chinese, was a one-two punch to the gut of the Chinese and African poachers. Some heard the word for snake in Arabic. This was a warning that the Mamba Patrol was here, if not near. The poachers were spooked by what they saw and heard, they froze.

What kind of curse would they bring upon themselves by destroying and defiling the jade elephants and silencing the holy sounds of an Arabic chant, the ominous word for snake, and even the word for jade in Chinese? Hearing the warning to leave and drop their guns immediately or face a counterattack added to the foreboding of the poachers.

By the grace of water beneath the ground and the hue of green vegetation above, and hearing the chants and warnings, the poachers couldn't shoot. Through their sight finders, they were mesmerized by the jade herd, the sound of the word jade in Chinese and the call to prayer. As the poachers retreated, they heard a voice booming from the sky, "Protect, Not Poach…Let the elephants go!"

Summation of the final scene in Lake Chad:

> *The poachers stopped cold. They could not betray their reverence for the call to Allah to bless life and for the power of jade to protect life. African and Asian culture and faith save the bedazzled jade elephants.*

Background and Source Material

Lake Chad
https://en.m.wikipedia.org/wiki/Lake_Chad
African Parks Organization and Mamba Patrols
https://www.bbc.com/news/world-africa-42367560 - African Parks, Mamba Patrol in Chad, partner with govt private, increase wild animals, elephants
Arabic for God and Life
Source: Adam Kliczek, http://zatrzymujeczas.pl (CC-BY-SA-3.0), https://commons.wikimedia.org/w/index.php?curid=29892612
If you mean by life as a synonym of existence, that would

be "الحياة" pronounced "Al Hayatte" or you can pronounce it " AL Haya " however the second proposition if not pronounced well could mean a "Snake", so i suggest to use the first one to be more clear.

The word "Life" can also be used as synonym of the word "Soul" or "Spirit", in this case the Arabic word would be "الروح" = "Al Rouh"

The Classical Arabic spelling of 'حَيَاة' is 'حَيْوة'. They are both pronounced the same.

Some answers stating that if you don't add the prefix 'al-' before the word 'حَيَاة' (ḥayāh), or that if you don't pronounce it as 'ḥayat' with a 't' sound at the end, that you will be instead saying the word 'snake'. The word for snake is 'حَيَّة' (ḥayyah). The only way the two words could be confused is if you don't pronounce the second vowel 'a' as 'ā', as in 'fār'. and instead pronounce it as 'á', as in 'fát'.

Boko Haram

The **Islamic State in West Africa** or **Islamic State's West Africa Province** (abbreviated as **ISWA**[13][14] or **ISWAP**),[15][16][14] formerly known as **Jamā'at Ahl as-Sunnah lid-Da'wah wa'l-Jihād** (Arabic: جماعة أهل السنة للدعوة والجهاد, "Group of the People of Sunnah for Preaching and Jihad") and commonly known as **Boko Haram**[17] until March 2015,[18][19] is a jihadist militant organization based in northeastern Nigeria, also active in Chad, Niger and northern Cameroon.[8]

CHAPTER 4

HOW THE HUNTED RHINO GOES GREEN

Raj the rhino was making his way through the forest in India. The one-horned rhino native to India, like their horns, have a singular mission to live in harmony with the environment around them. They are unique to the world living in the forests of India. Raj was a little on edge, its horn make it a target for poachers that go after it for its aphrodisiac qualities. Raj's bust is also prized by some in Asia, and China, in particular. They provide demand and the market for sexual vigor potions made of ivory, much as Viagra and Cialis pharmaceuticals are popular in North America. In fact, Elle - the elephant, also has to be aware of those targeting its tusks for the same reason. Elle knows this firsthand because she has grieved for one of her brothers taken by the poachers for its tusks. Indeed, Elle is the queen of emotional empathy for herself and others in its herd. Tenzin the Bengal tiger - also native to India and areas next to the Bay of Bengal - it's namesake, must be on the watch for farmers threatened by its presence and those wanting its skin for religious symbolism and as a decorative carpet. Tenzin is smart with his clever ways of surviving in a forest that is ever shrinking.

This uniquely Indian threesome were all in the same area on this bright day. The verdant green forest was beckoning the trio and visitors to enjoy its greenery. People from the neighboring villages rode in on elephants to collect plants for dyes and bright colors. As soon as they started their search, they kept their eyes peeled for hummingbirds. They will lead them to the right plants. They are beacons for flowers that have the ingredients for bright dyes. The- hummingbirds are built with eyes that can find the brightest of flowers to pollinate.

Just days away, India was about to celebrate the day that gave the world the name for some of people's most favorite days each year - 'Holiday'. Yes - 'Holi' day was approaching. On Holi, Indians of all faiths, economic means, and caste classifications play - abandoning egos and foolish pride - and bathe in colors splashed on them by friends and neighbors. Bongs made with plants also sprinkle the Holi parties to add to the relaxed and celebratory quality of the day.

Each year plants provide prosperity for those that gather the dye-making ingredients for the throwing of colors. Ganesh - the elephant god is an ancestor of Elle. She, is a direct descendant of Gajendra, Indian name for the elephant king. Ganesh promises abundance and the ability to overcome obstacles.

Nature provides the ingredients used to celebrate Holi and money for those who gather and sell the renewable goods.

The Holi gatherers of color that were on the ground, got startled. Tenzin, the tiger, roared to alert Raj the rhino; and Elle and her elephant herd. Elle also trumpeted selflessly to warn her herd that poachers were in the midst. The gatherers spilled much of the ingredients of green dye on the bushes around them. The strangers from Asia were trolling the forest for the threesome. The green dye splashed on the bushes as the gatherers rushed to find safety. Raj became a bright green rhino. But the strangers heard and then spotted the bright ones. The greenery that makes for a prosperous harvest also was on the side of the field - cut away to prepare the fruits and vegetables to be sold to marketing stores like Fresh Juice. Families from the area were having big feasts to celebrate the abundance of the harvest. The farms had Mango leaves in large piles on the side of the fields.

Ganesh as he is known in North India or Vinay as he is known in South India - promises abundance for those that honor his principles for receiving prosperity. And Kali or Durga, the Hindu god, rides upon a tiger and together they bravely protect the peace of mind of people and animals that share India.

Tenzin acted bravely to warn the rhino and elephants that poachers were on their trail - and they were about to be shot. He also had put himself in danger of being poached by the same hunters. The herd of elephants, and Raj the rhino, hearing the

29

warning roar from Tenzin - raced through the forest and even into the neighboring fields of the farmers to get away from the poachers. The strangers from Asia that were trolling the forest, followed the beaten trail of the elephants and rhino.

The greenery on the side of the fields from the harvest almost made the elephants look like they were wearing clothes. Elle charged through the mango leaves and green branches to get away from the strangers. The herd of elephants had become a regal troop of Green 'Jade' Elephants.

Raj however was closer and was in the hunter's sight, and the elephants were visible in the distance. The hunters took aim with their rifles. Instead of firing, however, they lowered their rifles. They had never seen such a magnificent jade rhino. To eliminate this 'gem,' would be a curse. As the strangers retreated, the Green Rhino and other witnesses spread the news. Eventually, Prince William, the Royal Patron of Tusks, and famous athletes - David Beckham of England and Yao Ming of China contracted green fever. Ming had already a taste that this would be his cause because he knew that in China the Shang Dynasty from 3700 years ago had revered a rhinoceros that once roamed in China. A famous urn now on display at the Asian Art Museum in San Francisco, California honors the rhino and has become green due to its Bronze origin.

Sadly, though, in Africa, the West African Black Rhino was declared extinct 8 November 2013.

The strangers moved on and spotted the bright green ones with their tusks and they saw another chance to earn money.

Awestruck, however, they lowered their rifles, again. The jade green elephants looked like a herd of Ganesh. The elephant god happens to be the most popular divine being revered in south Asia, and by deduction, the whole world. To eliminate these powerful and regal beings would be a bad omen. Instead, the jade green elephants decked in garlands from the leaves and branches that were on the sides of the field continued their walk in the field.

and The *Game arOZe*

This story and the others in the Arising series are meant to be 'evergreen'. It is meant to live on with other endings as well, created by readers and listeners. This applies especially to stories with a 'Jade Brigade' such as Raj and Elle's herd from this story, *How the Rhino Goes Green*. If you create a new ending or have input and insights please send it to soulpal.amp@gmail. com and you will be recognized on the 'Arising Breakthrough Network' at http://bit.ly/Rise-on. You will be acknowledged for your twist.

These endings will provide options for people that experience this as a game formatted to use Augmented Reality and Virtual Reality. This enables players to act through Avatars in the field with the rhino, tiger, and elephants and hummingbirds and the Holi makers.

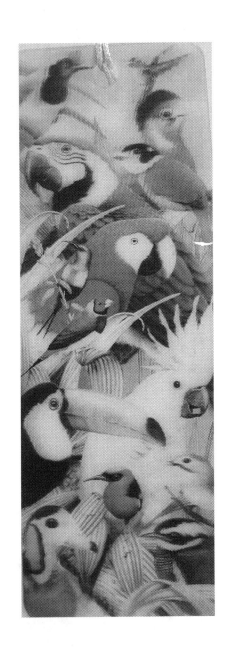

CHAPTER 5

BREEZE OVER BRAMAZON

(NOTE: You can read a more colorful and graphic version with related updates of this by clicking on or pasting in your browser, http://bit.ly/icBreezeDisruption)

Scene 1. Fade-in: Waves of heat shimmer on the pavements of the Manaus, Brazil airport in the heart of the Amazon. Manaus is teaming with activity as the central location for all things coming to and out of Brazil's Amazon. The Bramazon region is accessible only by a two-day Amazon river ride from Manaus. A motorboat scoots up the wide Amazon. It is on its way to the Bramazon region with Robin Steel, CEO of Wekia, a furniture maker, and the executives of PattyQueen (PQ), a fast food chain. Once in Bramazon, they will survey the region by horse.

On the way all are startled by a large splash of which they only see the remnants on the water's surface. Most likely it was a crocodile, but they couldn't be sure, as the Amazon teams with animals and water life of all sizes. Given the splash footprint on the river, it might be the pink river dolphin that lives and swims in the Amazon from Ecuador to Bolivia to Peru to Brazil. But it is rarely seen, and some wonder whether it is just an Amazon river myth.

Wekia has identified a massive Brazilwood grove to supply them their hardwood needs for years to come. Supporting this effort is PattyQueen (PQ), a fast food chain that sees the land to be cleared of trees, as a perfect place to raise cattle. The cows will be raised for dairy and beef to satisfy the appetites of its meat eaters and ice-cream lovers around the globe.

Scene 2. In Bramazon, the length of a Brazilwood tree is panned to the top of the rainforest canopy and then scans an unending sea of Brazilwoods.

In one Brazilwood tree, the inhabitants scurry and fly up the trunk to share a branch. Pride, the golden Lion monkey (Tamarin) feasts on some fruit and Brio, the Blue Macaw (Arara Azul) cracks a nut. They wonder if their house tree mate Hummer, (Beija Flor - Kiss of the Flower) will be flying in shortly. Hummer has been away on his yearly migration to North America since April. Hummer leaves in Brazil's fall, to suckle and pollinate at the blossoming flowers in North America. It's now October.

Scene 3. The Hummingbird annual migration for nectar and to pollinate goes from Bramazon, Brazil to Charlotte, North Carolina, U.S.A.:

Hummer and it's Beija Flor family is remarkable for its intelligence and advanced consciousness. Like a great yogi, Hummer is efficient with its energy and slows down its metabolism in the evening as it sleeps. This being has incredible mobility powers; it is able to hover and fly backwards. It has an extraordinary vision in the color spectrums to detect flowers for which it pollinates.

In his recent migration north, Hummer visited a 'Bird of Paradise' plant that he visits each year in Charlotte, North Carolina. Lotus Luv, a journalist, was visiting from Oklahoma. As a Native American, her parents gave her a name with a meaning to respect all of her relations on her upward spiral.**Her name is a mantra made of the letters of the name Lotus Luv (Live On The Upward Spiral (LOTUS), Love (the) Upward Vortex (LUV).

Luv was in a garden preparing to meet her interviewee. She had just lifted the 'bird of paradise' bloom to enjoy its fragrance. When she reached into lift the flower, Hummer was startled and pushed backward. He nearly bumped into the CEO of Wekia, with whom Luv was about to interview.

As Hummer 'kisses flowers,' he pollinates and multiplies them. Although a hummingbird weighs between two and eight grams (a penny weighs 2.5 grams), they eat frequently in order to power hearts that pump 1,200 times per minute and wings that beat seventy times each second. To survive, they must eat several times their weight in nectar every day! For protein, they supplement their sugary diet with small insects.

The Hummingbirds are the original intelligence for Global Positioning Systems (GPS). Revered as experts in pinpointing global destinations to the size of a plant from thousands of miles away, Beija Flor is mystically depicted in ancient Peru's landscape where their picture is sketched on the ground and visible only from space.

After nearly being slammed to the ground by Luv, Hummer was attempting to re-gain his balance.

He was hovering and just about to reverse course when he heard the words, 'A sea of Brazilwoods in Bramazon.' Luv, an agriculture journalist, was interviewing Wekia's CEO. Hummer continued to eavesdrop.

Robin Steel, Wekia's CEO, forecasts growth in the timber sector of industrial farming. Hummer got wind of their discovery of a gigantic stand of Brazilwoods. This would supply enough hardwoods to make furniture to fill the houses of the globally expanding middle class in China, Brazil and the U.S. Steel said they are just about to finalize the deal.

As Luv was completing the interview, she typed on her smartphone a note to investigate the impact of industrial farming, especially timbering and the raising of cattle for beef, on the global environment. She had heard a graduate of North Carolina State and an Indian Nobel-prize winner say that farming for meat was the biggest danger to the global environment.

Hummer Returns to Treemates in Bramazon, Brazil

Hummer after being welcomed back, summoned his treemates. He told them their home was being surveyed as a place for massive timbering and thereafter the grazing of cattle. The Brazilwood tree they lived in was in the path of the Wekia expansion.

Pride simply summoned the courage of his lion ancestors to protect and provide for their home. Even in the minds of many people, a lion is the symbol of courage. This is true in the Wizard of Oz. Pride thought, "Enough! This agricultural development without foresight cannot be allowed to proceed".

Pride then called a meeting of all of the members of his home. With Brio, an Azul Arara (Blue Macaw), the king of empathy, Pride thought it would be a sure-fire way to build a powerful coalition to halt the plans of Wekia. Amazonian beings from the river were brought into the cause as Pride tracked down the Rosa Boto (Pink Dolphin) to add power to the campaign. Azul Araras are known to mimic the sounds of other birds to draw attention and receive protection. This striking level of empathy used for the benefit of itself and others was the perfect motivator for this campaign. Pride also brought Brio - the Azul Arara, to the table because of its ability to review the situation and crack hard nuts, LOL. This mindless development is one such nut, thought Pride. Due to Hummer's intelligence, the hummingbird would lead the coalition to protect and preserve Bramazon.

Hummer, in the lead, called for a "Pollination Protest." From birds to bees, all pollinators in North Carolina would boycott pollinating plants. Hummer aimed to pressure Wekia to halt their plan, as growth in crops, gardens, and parks would shrivel all around. Maybe the company and its neighbors would get the message, to remove themselves from the Amazon. The Bees had initiated such a protest a few years back. At the time, journalists, Lotus Luv and Time magazine reported a massive decline in pollinating bees. (See the Time magazine cover in Notes online at http://bit.ly/icBreezeDisruption)

Woody, the Brazilwood tree, rested firmly planted on the floor of the rainforest. She provides shelter for all of these beings and was feeling hopeful that her home could be saved.

The coalition to save the forests, especially its home in a massive stand of Brazilwoods has succeeded. The trees were in danger of being slashed for the furniture of many in other lands and to fill their stomachs with cows and beef. This movement for 'Just-us for All' has grown with the successful outreach to other beings that live within Bramazon and those that love justice and the rainforest. Brio dropped leaflets throughout South America and Hummer's fleet has dropped fortune cookie sized slips with the protest website geared to North America, http://bit.ly/Just-usforAll. Brio and the Macaws have spoken to others. Humans have joined the environmental "Just Us" coalition's campaign cacophony to support a living rainforest, so the earth and all of its inhabitants can, 'Just Breath, it is Just Us (Justice) – those that need air' and to reverse the destruction of the Amazon. Amazingly nearly one-half of all rainforests are in the Brazilian Amazon and 20% of the oxygen we breathe comes from the rainforest.

The 'Just Us' Campaign by the treemates in the Brazilwood tree in Bramazon was so successful that it is the basis of this mural on a home in the U.S.A. The Just-usforAll campaign continues to root out injustice to people, animals, and the environment. See http://bit.ly/Just-usforAll

Word is out that the coalition is about to hear that the Brazilwood groves and indeed the entire ecosystem of Bramazon is to be preserved and made 'resilient.'

CHAPTER 6

THE FLYING RHINO

<u>Click</u> https://bit.ly/RhinoInFlight for the most updated, colorful, and pictorial *Flying Rhino*

Lotus Luv chief agri-business journalist from the state of Oklahoma in the United States of America stepped off the plane in New Delhi, India. Oklahoma (OK) state's motto is, "Labor Conquers All Things". She was alarmed because the people working in her state were in danger of losing their jobs or endangering everybody else. She had arranged to interview <u>Dr.Rajendra K. Pachaurithe</u>, the chair of the governing council of India's National Agro Foundation and chair of the United Nations' Intergovernmental Panel on Climate Change (IPCC). Coming from the breadbasket of the world, she had been jarred by Pachaurithe saying the meat industry is the largest sector emitting greenhouse gases. Credible scientists agree that the raising of cattle for consumption contributes to human induced global warming. Luv heard this while visiting North Carolina

State University at Raleigh. Pachaurithe is a graduate of North Carolina State University and was speaking on climate change.

Pachaurithe statements contradict the Oklahoma U.S. Senator, James Inhofe - a senior member of the Republican party on the U.S. Senate Environment and Public Works Committee. Inhofe denies that human contributions to climate change are causing global warming. A self-proclaimed authority he has written his own fiction. *The Greatest Hoax: How the Global Warming Conspiracy Threatens Your Future.* The Senator refuses to believe that global warming even exists. Eugene Takle, Professor of Agricultural Meteorology at Iowa State University said that "Farmers say they don't believe in climate change, but you look at how they spend money and (they) are adapting to climate change." Oklahoma's jobs are tied to the well-being of the cattle industry, and oil and gas extraction. Together, these are the largest business sectors contributing to carbon rising in the earth's ozone. Heat bounces back to earth from carbon and other greenhouse gas particles, heating the earth. Luv decided to visit Pachaurithe in India to probe this question.

As she exited New Delhi's express subway from the airport, Luv whistled for a taxi and everything on wheels seemed to be coming at her: sports cars, auto-rickshaws, horse drawn two-wheel carts, and bicycle pedal driven rickshaws, person-driven rickshaws.

She finally reached her hotel passing through a bustling market and trade center in the old part of New Delhi. After taking a rest and shower, Luv ventured into the streets to locate the site for her interview. She hailed a taxi. This time the variety of ways to travel expanded to disbelief. But she is in India and as they say, Incredible India, the unbelievable happens.

And then everything seemed to come-up elephant. An elephant trunk swayed from from side to side, the driver yelled, "Taxi?" And the elephant's eye and ear captured the stare of Luv's eyes. She had just landed in a country shaped like the right ear. She had also just completed a story about Brazil's Amazon, she saw the shape of both Brazil and South America in the flapping left ear. Africa - another continent is also shaped as an elephant ear. Even the Southeast United States with North Carolina being the Northern boundary and Florida as its tip-had the same shape as the elephant's ear. "Hmmmm, ears," Luv wondered to herself. The globe seems to come-up elephant. Everywhere she thought about and looked was in the shape of an elephant's ear. See what Luv sees at http://bit.ly/RhinoInFlight, p.3.

She considered taking the elephant taxi. Having light luggage, she said, "Why not!" She climbed up on the elephant - she felt like she was being buckled in to ride on the earth. She grabbed the seat tight, feeling like she just might fall-off.

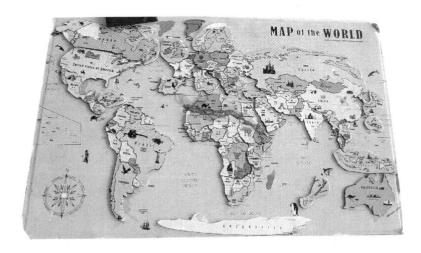

Luv was being taken for a ride beyond belief. By the time she arrived just beyond the city center, she was in a place that can only be seen in India. Nature and cities collide with all beings sharing the space. It was a watering hole and there among them were several other elephants.

A huge splash and commotion broke-out where the elephants were showering with water from their trunks. Luv was transfixed by an elephant in the herd. The ears again drew her in. There they were again, continents of the world walking on all fours. The elephant had become home, the earth. Under the water, a crocodile tip-toed to the four massive legs that rose from the floor of the river. The crocodile crept beneath the water with only a few bubbles rising to the surface and two eyes. With a splash the crocodile's jaws shot out of the water to snap onto the elephant's front leg. What had been peaceful, was now a full-blown emergency for the elephant. Luv felt her home on earth represented by the elephant, slipping away in the clutches of the crocodile.

Shocked into action, the rhino was overtaken by sadness for the elephant. However, with the forceful declaration, "to do something" by Lotus Luv, the rhino snapped back to the situation at hand. The rhino thought I must "Stop the Croc!" The rhino took command and commandeered a larger than life eagle, known as Garuda in India, to become its pilot. The rhino realized a straight on attack would only put her in death's clutches.

Luv pleaded with the eagle to help, sensing the desperation of the elephant. From on high, the eagle swooped down and became as large as a prehistoric bird. The eagle's back was large enough to be a saddle for the four-legged rhino. Situating herself below the belly of the rhino, two legs draped in front of the wings, and her two rear legs hung over the back of the wings.

With a massive effort, the eagle rose and stretched a wingspan larger than two-elephants. And up it went - a flying rhino. From above the watering hole, it circled and then did a direct dive to the front leg of the elephant. Just as the eagle was about to touch land, the rhino was let go and charged the crocodile with full speed and force. The crocodile's jaws were dislodged from the elephant's leg, and the force of the horn hitting the Crocodile in its tail flung the Crocodile 10 elephant lengths from the scene.

Lotus Luv was spellbound by the action before her eyes. She couldn't remember if she had already spoken with the chair of the IPCC, or had the scene in front of her been the interview? Had the Chair of the IPCC just told her the story of a carbon rising crocodile that had just threatened the life of the earth elephant. Were the elephant's ears pleading for her to just listen?

Luv was giddy with what she had just experienced. As a journalist, she wondered what should the headline be for her syndicated news story? Would any paper even run the story?

She returned to her hotel just behind the old market in New Delhi. Energized but famished, she wandered into the market that was festooned with neon lights, foods, books, school supplies, open air pastry and griller carts, clothing, and any and all goods that could be sold in the stalls. Autos, street cars, rickshaws - both peddled and human run, shared the road with carts led by cows and donkeys. She found some paper and pencils and drew what she had just witnessed.

After recording her observations, she posted them to her newspapers.

She recommended the headline be: Flying-Rhino defeats Carbon Rising Croc, the Earth survives. She posted it to her editors at the Oklahoman and the *Enid News & Eagle*.

Her editors have not run the story. On Google the story can not be found.

CHAPTER 7

OCTOPUS'S MAGICAL GARDEN (OMG): ALL TENTACLES READY TO ACHIEVE YOUR PINNACLE IN ALL REALMS

Coco the octopus and its 8 arms are here to lend helping hands to the two-leggeds (human beings and birds). Coco's eight tentacles built the magical garden as a place for sea beings to come together, help each other and protect where they live. For human beings, the pals of the garden can also inspire resilience.

Coco, in a dream, made it known that it's eight helping arms are coincidentally the same number that a land spider has to spin its web. An Octopus is really a water (H_2O) spider and catches all the meaning that comes with that dream.

Coco uses the water as its medium to amplify the powers within to spin your own web of reality.

As a longtime resident of Gulf Bay 'Coco'- the Octopus

cannot contain its admiration for the two-leggeds. Years ago, shipping was increasing, and development was happening all along the Bay. A few people said 'enough' to crowding out the sea life.

They protected Gulf Bay so this and future generations could enjoy it. Coco was inspired by the story of a diver that was so moved by the bludgeoning of a Giant Red Octopus on the shores of Seattle that he had the state of Washington in the U.S.A. pass a law protecting this type of octopus.

She partnered with humans to achieve protection from excessive cargo shipping and the degradation of her habitat from the exporting of gas. People recognized it for its beauty and started protecting the ecosystem. Coco's three Octopus-hearts pump ceaselessly with gratitude and a desire to give back to the two-leggeds for saving its home. Coco, as her partners call her, is quite remarkable in other ways. Coco uses coconut shells to hide and store food, so that it is ready on demand. Coco also reveals an important code that often goes unnoticed because it is below the surface of ordinary understanding. She hopes to inspire others to resilience, just as she has food resilience because she always keeps food hidden under a coconut that she keeps near her at all times. The PAL-Guide. at http://tinyurl. com/PAL-Guide describes how to decipher the code that is often subtle and below the service. And like other octupi, she can change her colors to best adapt to the environment. All and all, Coco is a perfect manager for the Octopus's Magical Garden (OMG).

With a treasure of gifts to offer and eight arms to lend a hand - the Octopus seeks ways to give to its cultivator residents all the tools to be expert cultivators. To make contact with the two-leggeds, humans and birds, the Octopus will introduce garden residents that can help replenish positive and diminish negative attitudes and actions (actitudes).

As wonderful as its sea gardeners are, the Octopus was wondering what to do to extend her reach beyond the underwater garden. Just then 'Brownie', a pelican and the state bird of Louisiana splashed-down. Brownie was searching for food before returning to the Park. The pelican was creating a refuge for birds and other creatures hoping to live despite the destruction of the largest oil-spill in world history. Aha, the octopus thought, the <u>pelican</u> and its <u>decisiveness and confidence</u> is the perfect messenger to bridge sea and land with its code.

The **OCTOPUS** as a Soul **PAL**
Soul **PAL**²: **P**ersonally **A**ctivate **L**iberty **&** **P**lay **A**t **L**ife

Pare Soul PALS with Attitudes and Actions (Actitudes) to CAPITALIZE and <u>underline</u> the nature of a Soul PAL to Replenish positive or Diminish destructive Traits at will.
All <u>underlined</u> words spell a Soul PAL and are formed by the letters of the Soul PAL word to be an empowering message such as:

The **OCTOPUS**'s **M**agical **G**arden **(OMG)**
Opportunity **C**enter **T**o **O**ffer **P**ractical & **U**seful **S**olutions

H_2O **SPIDER (another name for OCTOPUS)**
Homage $_2$ **O**neness
Stop **P**lanning **I**mpending **D**oom; **E**xperience, **R**eality
(-) Stop Planning for Impending Doom
and Exhausting Reality;
(-) Stop Preparing for Impending Doom
and Extinguishing Reality;
+ **S**tart **P**leasing **I**nternal **D**esires & **E**njoying **R**eality
+ **Sharing Passion Is DElight - Rendered!**

Ph +1 415-533-6210, About the Author: Hear an interview by StoryCorps, Library of Congress about the creation and intent of soul pals. Click and hear AMP Interview on creation of soul pals or copy and paste into your browser: http://bit.ly/SoulPalStory For Visual soul pal headlines, see: http://pinterest.com/amplaying/soul-pals

CHAPTER 8

YOUR PLAYGROUND: THE PERIODIC TABLE OF HUMAN CONSCIOUSNESS

The Playground is found among the tentacles of your perceived reality. Coco's eight tentacles trace a vast array of options to grow by. The playground is a matrix matching a quality that you wish replenished or diminished to a Soul PAL to assist in manifesting your desire.

Ways to Play on the Playground

The *Arising Series* are stories nested in a way to create and use soul **pals** for your own benefit. It is all about Playing At Life and Playfully Activating Liberty by palling around with these characters. Playing PAL unleashes a mystical code to amp your life. The energy boost comes from Acronym Mantra Power embedded within each PAL. The way to play pal is to adopt and create them and then pal around with them. When you look under Coco's coconut you find the simplest <u>PAL-Guide</u> for how to Form a PAL.

The recipe is to take the spelling of the name of a PAL and develop a meaningful message by using each letter of the name as the first letter of words in an impact phrase, and repeatedly bump into it visually, and say the phrase to yourself and/or aloud! Remarkably what is being imagined, manifests.

Play **PAL** for unlimited personal growth and joy.

PALS are your palate to shape your reality. What follows are only the headlines of the following **PALS**, later stories, jokes, riddles and poems illuminate the meaning of these characters. The <u>underlined</u> words are a way to link to each PAL in real-time on a living and continuously updated website. By using amp – **A**cronym **M**antra **P**ower – you energize and power up your life. Repeatedly see and say the PAL and create a conscious groove in your mind. You will dance to these grooves and be the cause of your desired reality.

Play the headlines of these five kinds of PALS, they are mantras to create your desired reality. By playing you will amp your life. The *Arising Stories* give meaning to PALS who are CAPITALIZED in this chapter.

1. **P**eople PAL (peo**PAL**) –
   CELIA: **C**aring **E**ntails **L**iving **I**n **A**wareness
2. **A**nimal PAL (ani**PAL**) –
   OWL – **O**pportunities **W**on't **L**inger

3. Living objects (**PAL**-it) –

   BED: Be **E**nlightened **D**aily, "You can be what you see." and

   PAL-ates – foods, "You are what you eat, you are what you repeat".

4. **S**pirit **PALS** - Flying **RHINO**:

   Raising **H**umor **I**nspires **N**atural **O**penness;

   Rise - **H**one - **I**nfiltrate - **N**ail – **O**vercome

5. Play 'Game arOZe' to bring these character's influence and power into your life. The game aroze from the *Arising Series*. Play PAL and win for yourself and others by AMPing life with soul pals. Members of the 'Jade Brigade' in the *Arising Stories* host 3Q in Game arOZe.

The game of life is on for all of us. We are on an upward spiral with the soul pals beginning from the depths of the sea in the **O**ctopus's **M**agical **G**arden and rising to the highest of heights - on the wings of a Flying Rhino see at http://bit.ly/ RhinoInFlight. Each successive story has moved one step up on the upward spiral, a metaphor as we rise in our own life.

From the garden, the Octopus has catalogued these characters in the following Periodic Playground of Consciousness so you have access to them on demand and at will.

In Chapter 1, the WOLF PACK, and PANDA become residents in the Pelican Park. Each in their own way helping the refuge become a home for all of its refugees. As an example, either: Click PELICAN1PAL

Or paste http://tinyurl.com/PELICAN1PAL into your browser - Use whichever way works.

What you can see, is crucial to receiving what you seek. A **pal**pable beat at the heart of successful **PALS** is the ease to see a picture of the PAL or imagine it in your mind's eye. Welcome to **PELICAN** Park and meet your host, an **A**nimal **PAL** (ani**PAL**) - the **PELICAN** pro**PEL**s confidence by affirming**I CAN**.

In Chapter 2: The EGRET struts with ease about its lagoon. Checking in with the pelican and WATER BUFFALO as it saunters about, as if it had arms whose hands were clasped behind its back.

Play the amp of the **EGRET** which is also a breathing exercise:

EGRET and EGRESS – *Don't Regret!*

Ease **G**ranted **R**elease **E**xcess **T**ension (**EGRET**) [breath in (inspire) deep for eight (8) seconds, hold six (6) seconds]
Ease **G**ranted (expire), **R**elease **E**xcess **S**tres**S** (**EGRESS**) [Exhale for eight (8) seconds

In Chapter 3:

The HIPPO shares Lake Chad with many other PALS whose names are code for messages to embody freedom, power, and confidence. See A Guide to PALS (http://www.tinyurl. com/PAL-Guide) of lake mates, such as CROCODILES, GIRAFFES, GORILLAS, and TIGERS.

Chapter 4: Meet the RHINO, HUMMINGBIRD, ELEPHANT, TIGER all part of the story. The rhinoceros and elephants are stars of the 'Jade Brigade'.

Chapter 5: Characters in *Breeze Over Bramazon*, include, LOTUS LUV, journalist, LION Monkey, a HUMMINGBIRD. And COW.

Chapter 6: In Flying Rhino, in the background, among the striped shade of the forest was a black and orange, Bengal TIGER PAL. Throughout this chapter, the CAPITALIZED phrase is also the link discovered by placing these capitalized words after "http://bit.ly/CAPITALIZEDWORD or by going to http://tinyurl.com/Propelling-Confidence, p.8. He was in the state of West Bengal which gave him his name. A couple of the elephants waded into a pool of knee-high water. A single-horned RHINO-PAL, native to India, was also at the watering hole. An EAGLE PAL circled above surveying the watering hole for prey.

Chapter 7: OMG in the Octopus's Magical Garden you have met Coco, the OCTOPUS managing her resident cultivators that are in this "Periodic Playground Table" that Coco has arranged and preserved under her coconut.

Enjoy the

Soul PAL

<u>Periodic Playground of Consciousness</u>
<u>Click</u> to Enjoy a more colorful story of the playground
at http://bit.ly/PeriodicPlaygroundofConsciousness

What follows is a table describing How to Play PAL and find
PALs relevant to you on life's playground. In scientific terms,
it is called The Periodic Table of Human Consciousness!

ACTITUDE*	Play PAL	Video PALS	Source documents
*Joining desired attitudes to actions	*PAL each day using your life as a palette to create your day.*	**P**eo-pal, **A**ni-pal, **L**ife-objects **S**pirit pals	**http://tinyurl.com/+**
	From waking-up		**+**
By PALling	*on pal-its, to eating pal-ates, and visually*	**See at http://** **www.youtube.**	**propelling-** **confidence**
Identifying **Problem**	*bumping into PALS in your PAL-ace, you will be loving each*	**com/watch?v=+** **+**	**e.g.**
+ Taking **Action by**	*moment more and more and realizing your dreams.*	X4eJg3q_QZQ	http://tinyurl.com/ propelling-confidence
Focusing on a **PAL to cause**		e.g. www.youtube.com/ watch?v=X4eJg3q	
Liberation			
Actitude	Soul PAL	Video PAL http:// www.youtube. com/watch?v= +	Web PAL http:// tinyurl.com/ +

How to Play at Ease with soul pals A story of an Upward Spiral	Play soul pal Origin of the Green Rhino, and the Game arOZe (originally E3OZ)	http://tinyurl.com/ SpiralPALate	PlaySoulPAL
Enjoy just being	BUZZ BEE (Anipal)		EZBEE
Confidence	PELICAN (Anipal)	PELICAN1PAL	Propelling Confidence
Awareness	CELIA (Peopal)		Letter C: in EZBEE
Persistence	APPLE (PAL-ate)		Letter A: in EZBEE
Overcoming Obstacles	CROCODILE (Anipal)		p.10 - PAL-Guide
Honesty	Abe (Peopal)		p.8 - PAL-Guide
Gratitude over Envy	GORILLA (Anipal)		p.1 - PAL-Guide
Leaping over problems	KANGAROO (Peopal)		p.4 – Propelling-Confidence
Stylishness & Creativity	IRIS (Peopal and Pal-it)		p.7 – Propelling-Confidence
Abundance	RABBIT (Anipal)	Singing Rabbit https://www.youtube.com/watch?v=T8EDG_OBcL4& feature=youtu.be	
Listening and being serene	ELEPHANT SEAL (Anipal)	pzHdF4r7IGQ& feature=share&list	
Resilience	TIGER (Anipal)	Singing Tiger https://www.youtube.com/watch?v=T8EDG_OBcL4& feature=youtu.be	p.8 - PAL-KIT

Jade Brigade: Stories of characters endowed with power from cultures and countries around the world and that become Jade. They serve as stewards for a way for us to playfully create a healthy personal and global experience - free of excess global warming and filled with fairness. See http://bit.ly/InvitationforJust-us			
OCTOPUS's Magical Garden (OMG)	Gardeners: octopus, sea horse, leaping bull frog, turtles, crocodiles	THE STORY http://bit.ly/ OMGWarNoMo	VISUALLY DISCOVER PALS IN THE STORY http://pinterest.com/ amplaying/soul-pals
Jaded In The Forest of Lake Chad	Lake Chad residents: Yemaya – baby elephant hippo – the hippopotamus rhino mambo patrol	http://bit.ly/ JadedinLake ForestJust-us	http://pinterest.com/ amplaying/soul-pals
Green Rhino: *How the Rhino Goes Green* Origin of the Green Rhino	in the field: green rhino, elephant, and tiger (anipals)	http://bit.ly/ RhinoJust-us http://tinyurl.com/ SpiralPALate	http://pinterest.com/ amplaying/soul-pals
Flying Rhino:	flying-rhino, eagle, elephant and crocodile, (anipals) and Lotus Luv (peopal)	http://bit.ly/ RhinoInFlight and http://tinyurl.com/ SpiralPALate	http://pinterest.com/ amplaying/soul-pals

Breeze over Bramazon	brio - the blue macaw, hummer - humming bird (kiss of the flower), pride - golden lion monkey & Brazilwood Tree	http://bit.ly/ icBreezeDisruption	http://pinterest.com/ amplaying/soul-pals

CHAPTER 9

GUIDE TO CREATING AND PLAYING SOUL PALS

Two **pals, Lotus Luv** and your **bed** let you 'awaken' each day in a **pal**ace of your own making and to a vortex of power made of your own experiences.

Lotus Luv is a journalist and observer in *Breeze Over Bramazon* and *Flying Rhino*. She is a peo**pal** (people pal) and she can be with you at anytime. She is easy to find when you are in an up mood and harder to find when you are in a low mood. Luv lives her name's amp and shows there's always a way to be on the rise and stop, pivot and reverse downward spirals. She reminds us that each of us is on an upward path, where we can flourish to the fullest. In the spirit of the Bee pal, "Float like a butterfly, sting like a bee." Mohammed Ali. Keep your eyes on the rise. We can be heroic having an amazing impact on each other and the world.

PLAY PAL: MEET IHE O-W-L ANIPAL.

This animal pal takes a perch in your mind and reminds you that **O**pportunities **Won't** **L**inger. The OWL reminds us to make wise choices by considering all related factors and choosing the best one, in order to fully enjoy yourself. Owls have the whole picture. They can survey 360 degrees of their surroundings with a swivel of their head. Perhaps, owls are thought of as wise because they go about their life with the full picture. They wisely see their opportunities, even peering in the darkness of night. We also can learn to get our own big picture. It is only from this vantage point that we can survey our choices and seize the best opportunities available; after all, Opportunities Won't Linger.

Becoming acquainted with a pal, such as owl, can help release many foul thoughts and embrace the way you really want to be. Negative programming can come from parents, friends, co-workers, or the myths repeated on TV and in the media about ourselves. Although these negative messages may not be intended, they attack the belief that we have in ourself, in our self-worth, in our intelligence, in our ability to complete goals and go after what we really want in life. Often these messages become so ingrained in our mind that we end up believing them, and as a result, limit our own personal expression and potential. Anipals (animal pals) like the owl are aimed at re-awakening inner awareness. Animals live naturally and so can we by following our own individual nature.

PAL tale

I had just purchased a ticket to visit a spectacular waterfall in the midst of a plush green rainforest in southern Mexico. This was a once in a lifetime chance to go deep into the rainforest, I had always dreamed of being in the rainforest and experiencing its people and beauty. I reserved a room for three nights in a town that was the marketplace of four indigenous villages. This would be my base camp. But after a day in one of the villages, I feared that I would see the culture as if on a TV set and not really be in it or get to know some of the people.

I went to dinner at a cultural center and house. While setting the table for dinner, I tried to make conversation with a young man who appeared to be from the area. All of my greetings in the local dialect that I had learned that day, failed. I was discouraged and resorted back to Spanish, and to my surprise I learned that he was visiting from a remote village deep in the rainforest.

Wow! My heart raced. He hadn't responded to my greetings earlier because he spoke pure Mayan, not a local dialect. He had to return to his village that night. My O-W-L pal kicked into gear. Without delay, I immediately asked to join him on his trip home, and to my surprise he said yes. I seized the moment and immediately dropped my ticket to go to the waterfall and left my room that was still reserved in the town.

By midnight, we were on the highway flagging down a bus. Within 12 hours, I was hiking in the heart of the rainforest to a Mayan village that had been in existence since the invasion of the Spaniards in the 1400s. I later learned, this village is home to some of the 400 direct descendants of the Mayans whom had built the great pyramids in that area amid the Palace of Palenque.

Carmelita, the mother of the young man, who had brought me to the village is a magical woman of grace, serenity and dignity. She kept watch over a small cooking area, where three logs pointing toward each other formed a triangle that supported pots for cooking. At any moment, Carmelita could use her breath to ignite the glowing red embers. The fire burned when she desired it to cook. Pals are the warm red glowing embers of self-mastery. Like the OWL, when we focus on them, they ignite our personal greatness, creativity, and attention to the present moment. Pals prepare us to grab on to what we desire, when it arrives without delay. Wouldn't it be refreshing to playfully confront personal challenges and experience them as possibilities for growth, rather than taking negative messages to heart.

How liberating it would be to light our own fire and fine tune our perspective at our own command. The PALs embody a concept to do just that. Each pal is here for you to befriend. There are three kinds of PALs in this club for the soul. People Pals known as **P**eopals, Animal Pals known as **A**nipals, and **L**ife's Objects known as PAL-its. PAL works by attaching a special meaning to a word. A PAL word must be PALPABLE, something that a person can actually see with their eyes or imagine in their mind. It needs to be something that can be visually bumped into or pictured in your mind during the course of a day. We can create secret peopals (people pals) who we can call on at any time to support and re-assure us when we are having insecure and destructive thoughts.

For instance, ABE, who reminds us of the bearded Abe Lincoln, could become a peopal to help prevent us from being tempted to lie. Just by looking at a penny, we could consider, that to **A**lways **B**e **E**arnest makes good sense. If we live by this ethic, we would never have to waste mental energy on worrying about being found out for having not told the truth. Like the "palette" of an artist, the pal-its can be used to energize and form our attitudes and actions throughout the day.

A palette is a thing from which the artist creates the texture and color of a picture. Similarly, the pal-its are common objects in our life that can be used to create the texture and feeling for our day. Your mind is your Number " 1" PALace (pal plus ace). Imagine — a palace where all pal-its are furnished, so that each time you run across the object in the day you associate it with its special PAL meaning. When a word such as BED becomes an abbreviation or acronym for a special phrase, like "Be Enlightened Daily," it becomes one of the PALs. What would the impact be on your thinking, if from the moment you got out of BED, you associated everyday objects with thoughts like. Be Enlightened Daily? Each time you repeat a positive re-enforcing thought you are regaining perspective, countering negative messages, and returning to your own positive resilience.

PAL-ATE (The Food Pals) members of the PAL-IT group. Satisfy your personal palate. Satiate your hunger for individual courage, quench your thirst for being the way you want to be. "You are what you eat, You are what you repeat". If we attach personal meaning to a food pal, then every time that we eat it, we can be nourishing our body and an attitude that we wish to improve upon and experience. For instance, an APPLE might remind us that each of us is like a seed within an APPLE'S core. The seed must persist and release itself from the core to reach its full-grown potential - a full grown apple tree. We, too, must persist to reach our goals because **A**ctive **P**ersistence **P**revails **L**iberating **E**xpression. An apple a day, can keep your own dreams in play.

There are times where all you want to do is strike back, even take revenge, The CROCODILE pal can save you from unnecessary grief, and bring you relief.

Only eyeballs and nostrils breach the rivers surface, Danger lies ahead; an opponent wants crocodile slivers, On a boat there stands a hunter wanting him dead. Laughter will soon prevail, though, and not crocodile red, Employing a careful response, will stop the hunter's ego from being fed. The hunter stands with a rifle nestled on his shoulder. His eye waits and targets every movement. The hunter feels bolder and bolder.

C alm and quiet,

R eady to satisfy its diet,

O n an afternoon patrol,

C onfidently taking an underwater stroll, But the hunter only sees what's in front and in sight. From behind, the crocodile glides with quiet might.

He's not looking for a fight. Scanning the foreground - the hunter keeps his rifle cocked. Suddenly, the boat is rocked. The hunter is shocked, losing his rifle and balance in utter surprise.

The crocodile's smile rises to its eyes,

The hunter of demise wriggles back into the boat.

Leaving the scene without a sliver or even a gloat.

Now of course — you know, that opponents will try and rile.

They'll defile and they'll create a pile. All of it being nothing but a crock of vile. They want you to lower yourself and strike back. And they're spending energy waiting for your counterattack. Leisurely consider these barraters, The wait will frustrate these time invaders. Respond to these agitators. Occupy these alligators. Let them know, they'll see you later, Laugh quietly at their failed trial. Crack a smile. You're a clever crocodile. Not about to fall into their crack of vile.

Calm

Response

Occupies

Conniving

Opposition,

Denying

Intrusion;

Laughter

Empowers!

Calculated

Response

Over

Contrived

Opposition,

Diminishes

Influence, &

Limits

Exhaustion

PAL Tale:

We all face people with power trips and political games from people at work in our communities, and even in our family. A legislator and chair of a committee that oversaw a $50 billion budget was particularly frustrated. It had been two years of explaining and educating others about the importance of a proposal that had deep personal meaning and wide implications for the way priorities were determined in the budget. This year he had successfully received the needed votes in both chambers of the legislature, all he needed was the Governor's signature.

With nothing less than anguish, he received a letter from the Governor that denied the legislation from going into law. It was at this point that he brought his crocodile smile to bear. Rather than burn his bridge and berate this Governor, he calmly responded. The following year it passed and to everyone's surprise the bill was signed into law by the same Governor. It ignited a national effort to get to the root cause of various social problems and re-prioritize how we make social policy.

The PALs you have met and will meet demonstrate how to apply the PAL concept. Some PALs you may like and others you may not. In the end, what is most important is that you create or adopt PALs that best work for you.

The basic formula for forming your pals is described below:

First, a **P**roblem or challenge is identified as a possibility' for growth.

Next a pal for whom you already have a special feeling toward is chosen. Then this pal is **A**pplied to the problem by simply focusing on a picture of the PAL and thinking about this being. You then connect a phrase of words that begin with the letters that together spell a PAL word. These letters will embody a phrase or saying that has a special meaning to overcome the problem at hand. Gradually, the repetition of the visual image, its associated word meaning and the feelings you experience when bringing your pal to mind, will **L**iberate you from a thought that may have limited your ability to lead your life as you desire.

P-roblem identified

A-pplication of an AMPed PAL

L-iberation

Focusing on GIRAFFE - you might come up with this: **Go In Re**assured, **AFF**irmative, & **E**nthusiastic. Now - by looking at or thinking of this PAL all of the words that are embodied by the spelling of the PAL come to mind. By reminding yourself to go in with your head up high like that of a giraffe, you can help maintain some level of confidence in situations where you are meeting new people and interviewing. Such reminders build power within to change your ways and your attitudes. You are transforming negative headlines in your mind into positive ones. More and more you'll be believing yourself and be believing in yourself

PAL Tale:

I didn't have a permanent position in the company. I was a temporary working in the mail room. Admittedly, it's an awkward feeling. Everybody in the office seems to be so busy - there is little time to get a feel for whom I am working. The principal partner of this targe law firm doesn't help matters. He is a brisk and physically large and an imposing person. I noticed that he gets a real pleasure by intimidating others with his stare-down tactics. He'll look at you sternly, not to make contact but rather to see when you will turn away from his glare. I didn't feel comfortable around this, in fact I resented it. I was about to burst one day. I was seething inside because all day I spent avoiding the glance. At last, I decided enough is enough. I am fed up. I had to do something. My preferred choice is to be dignified, stand tall, and bounce back the intimidating glares.

I used GIRAFFE to be the way I wanted to be in this

new environment. The first time I faced the glare with my GIRAFFE pal in mind, my heart raced, my eyes didn't blink, and my head stayed up during the stare down: it was a victory of sorts. By the third time, the stare downs had ended, and I felt much more comfortable in the job. I carry myself differently as I envision the gracefulness of a giraffe galloping. Instead of grinning and bearing the insults, I am now grinning and daring.

HOW CAN YOU FIND YOUR BEST PALS?

When you see or even think about a PAL, whether it is a peopal, anipal, or pal-it, it should bring about some special feeling within you. Often this feeling can come about simply by creating your own pals. A gift given to you by someone important often evokes this warm sense of attachment about which I am speaking. Viewing a magnificent animal or a beautiful natural scene could also bring about this serene and refreshing sense. All of these are potential PALs. Jot down a couple of things, people, or animals that give you a feeling of happiness and well-being when you see them in your mind's eye. By playing with your PALs different areas of your life are transformed, and your desired attitudes and actions (actitudes) become as natural as your own heartbeat.

Play At Life

Play at ease,

Replenishing and Diminishing Personal action and attitude Traits.

PALling around Keeps you play bound.

Always growing,

Bringing to yourself more understanding and knowing,

Making your day brighter and lighter;

Life's a playground.

We can hide behind mounds

Then climb them and roll down.

We grow ourselves by playing lost and found.

Enjoy the PALs on your playground.

This is a mini playground of the PALs we have just met, includes PALs that we have already met and each actitude that they support:

- OWL – Carpe Diem,
- GIRAFFE – Confidence in facing intimidation,
- ABE – Honesty is best and easy compared to the energy used to hide things
- CROCODILE – Repel intimidation and prevail

There is strength in being the best you, rather than bowing to somebody's whims and judgements. PALs that have teamed up with various actitudes, ranging from arrogance to trust to zaniness are available. See the whole playground in the Periodic Table of Human Consciousness, Chapter 8.

CHAPTER 10

IMPACT INTENT OF THE ARISING STORIES OF SOUL PALS AND THE GAME AROZE

Arising Stories and the Game arOZe to achieve a world of compassion and action to realize a globe of healthy people, animals – all sentient beings, and a rejuvenated earth and all of it's ecosystem.

These stories arch in an 'upward spiral' and are powered by playing with the soul pals. It is the game of playing with the characters and their qualities that can help in elevating consciousness. This *Arising* journey emulates the power you have to choose your destinations on the upward spiral, at will. As we arise, each of us manifests our dreams. And when we get to those goals, we have aroze, from arising to aroze, is the upward spiral of our own creation.

The series begins from the depths of the sea visited by the

pelican and next rises to land with elephants in Africa being *Jaded in the Forest of Lake Chad* and then to the charging of a Rhinoceros in Northern India in *How the Hunted Rhino Goes Green*. The spiral continues upward to the sky with the hummingbird's yearly flight from Brazil to the U.S. and back, in *Breeze over Bramazon*. The highest of heights comes with the *Flying Rhino*.

By reading about the characters' three primary qualities of IQ+EQ+We-Q we arrive at **3Q** in the Game ar**OZ**e. By playing 3Q you win by expanding the Qs within. In the game you: 1. win prizes, 2. grow personally, and 3. understand what needs to happen for all to thrive in "our common home" here on earth.

The Jade Brigade characters convey the keys to unlock, unleash and raise the 3Qs just by playing with these pals. The 3Qs are:

1. EQ = Emotional Quotient giving love and compassion. In the stories, the star characters express their heart with love and care for each other, just as the Tin Man seeks heart as he skips down the yellow brick road arm in arm with Dorothy, the Lion and the Scarecrow in the *Wizard of Oz*.

2. IQ = Intelligence Quotient which measures the brain's skill to think and solve problems. The characters think up solutions to the challenges they face. They share the path of the Scarecrow to apply intelligence from their brains.

3. WE-Q = Tracks the Courage to do the right thing with all our relations. The characters act selflessly even though their own life is in danger. The Lion in the *Wizard of Oz* discovers his own courage and is recognized for it by the Wizard.

THE WIZARD OF OZ THREE STARS, THE SCARECROW, THE TIN MAN AND THE LION PURSUE THREE QUALITIES ESSENTIAL FOR LIVING.

By taking the journey in the *Arising* Series and playing the Game ar**OZ**e, the hope is that all feel growth in their own 3Qs. Stories and characters are drawn from North America (USA), South America (Brazil), Africa (Nigeria, Niger, Cameroon, and Chad), India and the Asian continent (China). These countries together, represent a majority of the world's population and economic activity. The goal is to draw new advocates to the cause of generating a healthy earth that prevails over global warming and poverty.

This is an impact project driven by 'playing pal' with the stories in *Arising* and the Game arOZe. Each story is based on true facts about people, nations, animals, culture and spiritual practices. <u>Disclaimer</u>: The names have NOT been changed to protect anyone.

The nature of the characters is the basis for the amp technique to 'play pal' and recognize, remember and uncover the best in each reader, listener and player. The soul pal technology fuses visual (pictures) and auditory senses (music) with emotional, intellectual and word cues to help remember and acknowledge how you shall live and what you shall achieve. The soul pals can help fully realize your potential. The Jade Brigade characters in the *Arising soul pals Stories* host the Game arOZe.

Game arOZe is being developed to go global on mobile phones, desktops. The game, 3Q will be featured along with AWAREables (wearables) as accessories to what you wear and carry. A PALendar is a calendar app to focus and meditate on Soul PALs during each day of the week. Game arOZe is described more fully at the completion of the online Periodic Playground for Human Conscious at http://bit.ly/PeriodicPlaygroundofConsciousness. The object is to play and win, and by doing so learn about yourself and "our common home "– the earth. Pope Francis coined the phrase "Our Common Home" in *Laudato Si'* (http://bit.ly/PraiseCreation), proclaiming praise for creation and creator, the earth and all that live upon it. The game's motto is *"Play - Because there is no place like home!"*

For live and updated Arising Stories, Soul PALs, and poetic insights see: http://bit.ly/Rise-on

Printed in the United States
By Bookmasters